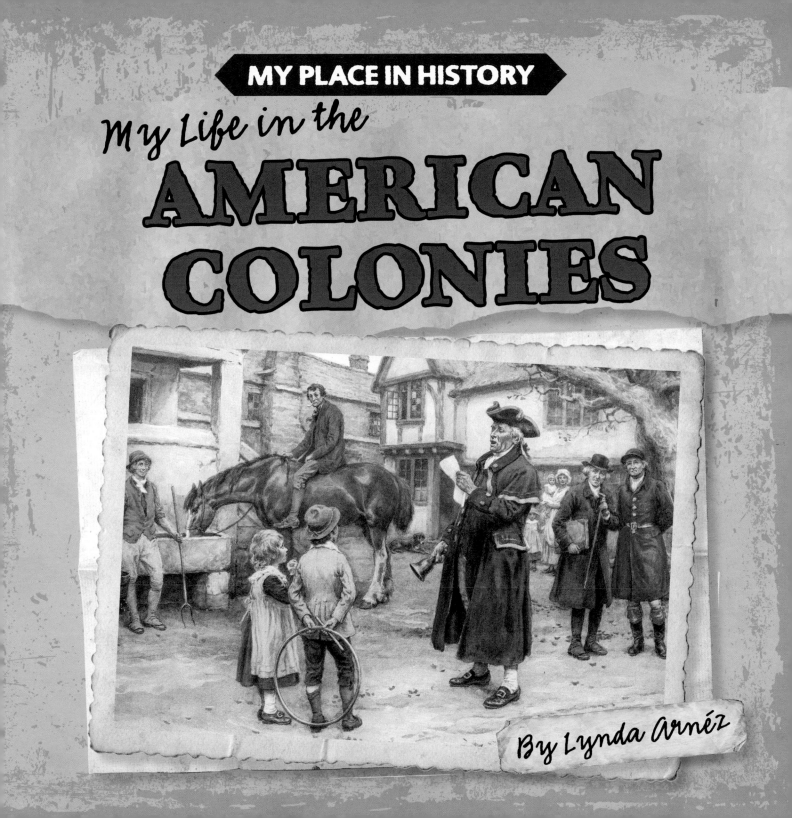

My Place in History

My Life in the
AMERICAN COLONIES

By Lynda Arnéz

Please visit our website, www.garethstevens.com. For a free color catalog of all our high-quality books, call toll free 1-800-542-2595 or fax 1-877-542-2596.

Library of Congress Cataloging-in-Publication Data

Arnéz, Lynda.
  My life in the American colonies / Lynda Arnéz.
    pages cm. — (My place in history)
  Includes bibliographical references and index.
  ISBN 978-1-4824-3992-2 (pbk.)
  ISBN 978-1-4824-3993-9 (6 pack)
  ISBN 978-1-4824-3994-6 (library binding)
  1. United States—History—Colonial period, ca. 1600-1775—Juvenile literature. I. Title.
  E188.A74 2016
  973.2—dc23

                                   2015026008

First Edition

Published in 2016 by
Gareth Stevens Publishing
111 East 14th Street, Suite 349
New York, NY 10003

Copyright © 2016 Gareth Stevens Publishing

Designer: Laura Bowen
Editor: Kristen Nelson

Photo credits: Cover, p. 1 GraphicaArtis/Hulton Archive/Getty Images; cover, pp. 1-24 (torn strip) barbaliss/Shutterstock.com; cover, pp. 1-24 (photo frame) Davor Ratkovic/Shutterstock.com; cover, pp. 1-24 (white paper) HABRDA/Shutterstock.com; cover, pp. 1-24 (parchment) M. Unal Ozmen/Shutterstock.com; cover, pp. 1-24 (textured edge) saki80/Shutterstock.com; cover (background) Natalia Sheinkin/Shutterstock.com; pp. 1-24 (paper background) Kostenko Maxim/Shutterstock.com; p. 7 Hulton Archive/Getty Images; p. 9 (main) Heritage Images/Hulton Fine Art Collection/Getty Images; p. 9 (inset) Print Collector/Hulton Fine Art Collection/Getty Images; p. 11 (main) Jorge Moro/Shutterstock.com; p. 11 (inset) Print Collector/Hulton Archive/Getty Images; p. 13 (main) DEA Picture Library/De Agostini/Getty Images; p. 13 (inset) GraphicaArtis/Archive Photos/Getty Images; p. 15 Three Lions/Hulton Archive/Getty Images; p. 17 Everett Historical/Shutterstock.com; p. 19 Universal Images Group/Getty Images; p. 21 Matanya/Wikimedia Commons.

Printed in the United States of America

CPSIA compliance information: Batch #CW16GS: For further information contact Gareth Stevens, New York, New York at 1-800-542-2595.

CONTENTS

Precious Paper. 4

In the Fields 6

Reading and Writing 8

Homecoming 10

Rebel Worries 12

Domestic Help 14

Teaching a Friend 16

Time to Play 18

An Independent Future? 20

Glossary. 22

For More Information 23

Index 24

Words in the glossary appear in **bold** type the first time they are used in the text.

precious PAPER

May 30, 1773

    Mother says I should be very thankful for this little book she's giving me. Just a few years ago, she said, there were laws that taxed paper and it would have cost a lot for me to have my own! I have four brothers and two sisters, so I *am* thankful to have a book that's just mine.

    My family lives in the colony of Maryland near St. Mary's City. We have a small farm and grow tobacco and some wheat.

Notes from History

During the 1700s, many colonial families lived on small farms. Since the whole family worked on the farm, having many children was helpful and common.

THE 13 COLONIES

ME

NH

NY

MA

CT

RI

PA

NJ

MD

DE

VA

historic St. Mary's City, Maryland

NC

SC

GA

In 1767, the British government passed the Townshend Acts taxing paper, tea, glass, and other common goods sold in the 13 American colonies. Colonists **protested** it, saying "no taxation without **representation**" and showing the growing unhappiness with British rule.

In the FIELDS

July 18, 1773

I'm so tired I can barely keep my eyes open! I was up at sunrise this morning to feed and give water to our animals before heading out to the fields.

My father **inherited** a slave family from his father, and they've lived with us my whole life. Now that I'm 9, I work right next to them, my father, and three of my brothers. Tobacco farming is hard, but my father says we make a lot of money from it.

Notes from History

While boys learned their father's work, colonial girls learned how to run a household from their mothers. They learned to sew, make bread, and care for younger children.

Before the **American Revolution**, all 13 colonies had slaves. In Maryland and other southern colonies, slaves were a big part of the workforce on the many tobacco farms and **plantations**.

Reading AND WRITING

October 1, 1773

Now that much of the **harvest** has been brought in, Mother and Father want me to spend more time reading and writing. There used to be a school near our farm that my older brother David went to. It's not there anymore, but he and my mother have taught me to read the Bible and write whatever I want.

Sometimes I go to the Millers' farm a few miles away to learn math. The Miller boys have a math **tutor**!

Notes from History

How much schooling colonial children received greatly depended on where they lived. It was common for both boys and girls to go to school for many years in New England, for example.

White families with more money could afford to hire teachers for their children.

HOMECOMING

December 20, 1773

Last night, my brother Jacob came home! He's an apprentice to our uncle who's a **blacksmith**. He's almost 16 and hasn't lived at home with us since I was a baby.

Jacob works in Baltimore and meets a lot of different kinds of people. He told David and my father that many people there don't want us to be British colonies anymore. They want us to be our own country! I think it sounds exciting, but Father and David didn't seem too happy.

Notes from History

An apprentice is someone learning a trade, such as printing or shoemaking, from a person already working in the trade.

Having a child work a trade could be just as helpful to a colonial family as having him work in the fields. He might be able to send earnings back to feed his family.

Rebel WORRIES

February 1, 1774

I found a letter to my father from my uncle in Baltimore:

My dear brother,

*As you may have heard now, a group of **rebels** dumped a shipment of tea into Boston Harbor on December 16. Jacob has been at meetings where men from the city are talking about revolution! I worry if more happens, Jacob will leave his apprenticeship here and take part in this movement. Please write and encourage him to stay out of it.*

I wonder why they dumped the tea.

Notes from History

The group who dumped tea into Boston Harbor were against the Tea Act, another law about tea taxes passed by the British government without any say from colonists.

Today, the Boston Tea Party is seen as one of the major events that led to the American Revolution.

Domestic HELP

March 20, 1774

It's raining hard today, so it's my job to help Mother and Martha in the house. Martha is what my mother calls "domestic help." That means Martha's a slave, but she works in the house. She helps Mother cook all our meals, clean, and wash our clothes. Martha took care of all my brothers and sisters when they were little. She still helps me because I'm the youngest.

Martha has children, too. Sam is the same age as me!

Notes from History

Some colonial families treated their slaves with kindness and even granted them freedom. However, most slaves were treated badly and forced to work in terrible conditions.

In many cases, domestic slaves became part of the family, especially since they often cared for children from birth. In many homes, slave children and white children played together during childhood.

Teaching A FRIEND

April 3, 1774

I've been teaching Sam to read and write since I learned how. I want him to be able to share books with me. I told him to write something here!

My name is Sam. I live with my family on a farm in Maryland. I started working as a field slave with my father and brother last year. It's hard, and I wish I could play more. When I was younger, I helped my mother in the house, carried water, and gathered firewood.

Notes from History

South Carolina had a law against teaching slaves to read and write in the 1700s. This became more widespread in the American South during the first part of the 1800s.

Slave families in the 13 colonies didn't often get to stay together. Strong men might be sold off as teenagers. Fathers sometimes walked late at night to see their family on other farms and plantations.

Time TO PLAY

June 3, 1774

Father says that I can go play! We worked all morning in the fields, and since we went fishing yesterday, he says we need an afternoon off.

My 10th birthday was last week, and I got a brand-new kite! I'm going to take it to the Millers' house and play with them until suppertime. Mother says she's cooking some of the fish Father and I caught with vegetables from our garden. I wouldn't want to miss that!

Notes from History

Children in the colonies often made their own toys, or their parents made them toys.

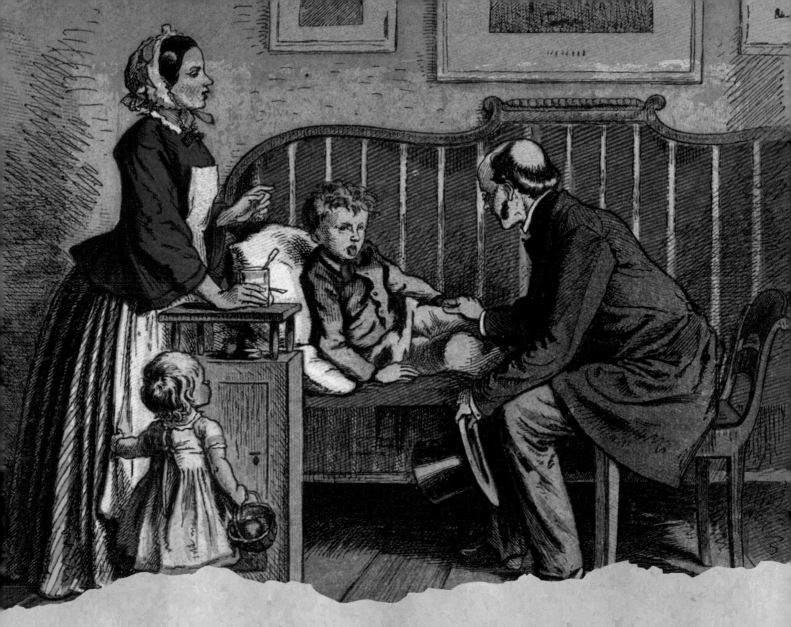

Many colonial children didn't live beyond birth. Those who did faced many illnesses, such as smallpox and the flu, that doctors didn't know how to treat at the time.

An Independent FUTURE?

August 18, 1774

My father received a letter from my brother Jacob today. He read it out loud to my mother, and I listened from the kitchen!

Jacob wrote that a group of men are gathering in Philadelphia next month. Many of them are fed up with the British laws. Jacob said he met one of the men going to represent Maryland!

I wonder what will happen in Philadelphia? How would my life be different if we weren't part of Great Britain?

Notes from History

The First Continental Congress met from September to October 1774. They wrote a list of **grievances** for the British king and said they'd meet again if the problems weren't fixed. They met again in May 1775—and agreed to a Declaration of Independence.

Events Leading to American Independence

June 29, 1767	The Townshend Acts go into effect.
May 10, 1773	The Tea Act goes into effect.
December 16, 1773	The Boston Tea Party occurs.
September 5 to October 26, 1774	The First Continental Congress meets and writes a list of grievances.
April 19, 1775	British troops and colonists fight at Lexington and Concord.
May 10, 1775	The Second Continental Congress gathers.
July 4, 1776	The Congress agrees on the final Declaration of Independence.

FIRST CONTINENTAL CONGRESS, 1774

GLOSSARY

American Revolution: the war in which the colonies won their freedom from England

blacksmith: someone who makes and fixes things made of iron

grievance: an objection

harvest: crops brought in from farmland

inherit: to get by legal right after a person's death

plantation: a large farm

protest: to show opposition

rebel: one who fights to overthrow a government

representation: the act of being represented, or having a person or group stand for a larger group, such as a colony

tutor: a teacher who instructs an individual student

For more INFORMATION

Books

Gagne, Tammy. *Life in the Original 13 Colonies.* Hockessin, DE: Mitchell Lane Publishers, 2016.

Pratt, Mary. *A Timeline History of the Thirteen Colonies.* Minneapolis, MN: Lerner Publications, 2014.

Sullivan, Laura L. *The Colonial Slave Family.* New York, NY: Cavendish Square Publishing, 2015.

Websites

Colonial Williamsburg Kids Zone
history.org/kids/visitUs
Find games, links, and information about life in the American colonies.

The Original Thirteen Colonies
congressforkids.net/Independence_thirteencolonies.htm
Review facts about the 13 colonies.

INDEX

American Revolution 7, 13

apprentice 10, 12

Boston Tea Party 13, 21

boys 6, 8

British government 5, 12, 20

children 4, 6, 8, 9, 11, 14, 15,
        18, 19

colony 4, 5, 7, 10, 12, 17, 18

domestic help 14, 15

family 4, 6, 9, 11, 14, 15, 16, 17

farm 4, 6, 7, 8, 16, 17

First Continental Congress 20, 21

girls 6, 8

illness 19

Maryland 4, 7, 16, 20

Philadelphia 20

plantation 7, 17

play 15, 18

school 8

slaves 6, 7, 14, 15, 16, 17

tobacco 4, 6, 7

Townshend Acts 5, 21